LAST DAYS ON EARTH

Layout and Book Design: DUSIE
dusie.org | Block Island, Rhode Island

First printing, 2019.

Written in daily downloads beginning on May 2016-August 2016.

ISBN: 978-1-944253-04-2
LCCN: 2019934173

LAST DAYS ON EARTH

JOE ROSS

DUSIE

LAST DAYS
ON EARTH

*for Julien and Juliette,
my source of Love Pulling*

This is left
    An old man sitting on a bench

A Cane
    Supporting the sun which will not support us

A Broken World
    In full repair

A Race
    Time itself, against time

Love Pulling
    Us to ourselves to see the waters rising,
    against water itself

Oh how you have tried, so hard, so tired

A Tide of Trends
    Documenting ourselves, against documenting itself

A Key
    Which opens something so far lost
    replaced by a code replacing itself

A Perpetual State
    Of just about to collapse
    as collapse fights desperately against itself

Love Pulling
    A female voice from far away
    becoming clearer, stronger, against silence itself

This is left
    A half-forgotten story and have remembered songs

A Music
    Made of the silence found between notes
    of time vibrating and marking a moment itself

A Making
    That is each now, that ever was ever will be
    you in constant construction, against construction itself

A Woman hugging a child
    On the grass in a daisy strewn park
    watching a boat taking water, taking time itself

A Swinging door
    On a rusted hinge shrieking open and closed
    outside and in, inside and out, interchangeability itself

A Balloon
    Half floating in dirty air drifting
    defying accepted truths like gravity, against gravity itself

A Shore
    Defined by the sea which has become a wall
    invisible and real, a single wave against singularity itself

Love Pulling
    The separation together stitching the fabric of want into
    the whole from which we became, against becoming itself

This is left
     A flag from some long forgotten country

A Camera
     Capturing an image of a disappearing flower
     desperate to bloom

A Cloud
     Carrying too much water to carry life itself

A Stain
     On a sidewalk outlined in chalk

Love Pulling
     Toward the outer bounds known as up
     heaviness letting go, against heaviness itself

Oh to be there at the end of time

A Root
     Reaching for connection, against connection itself

A Child
     Being passed hand to hand
     lifted from harm, against harm itself

Love Pulling
     A far away voice in urgent whisper
     growing louder, more insistent, again insistence itself

This is left
      An absence similar to lift lost in the dark

A Terrorism
      Made of the unseen like wind passing

A Wave
      That gives way to morning
      opening into a darkness against darkness itself

A Cause
      Being defined as purpose to push apart
      the visible as reason against reason itself

A Broken Stick
      Marking the path from a tree to last step
      taken without certainty against certainty itself

A Piece of glass
      Being crushed in the wide open house
      of mirrors hiding reflection from reflection itself

A Hat
      That has given up on being worn

Love Pulling
      The meaning from existence from extinction
       so near the cliff of time against time itself

This is left
	A rock on the ledge painted white

A Bag
	Filled with useless objects of connection

A Toy Truck
	Rusting in forgotten motion of play

A Gilded Belt
	Hugging tightly the last vestiges of hope

Love Pulling
	So close yet so far into deafness
	of resolution's purpose, against purpose itself

Oh what are the ways, of the way you have given up on

A Language
	Yet to be spoken but is speaking
	so clearly without words, against clarity itself

A Scarf
	Pulled from the head of a wearer
	lost somewhere in the desert defining lass itself

Love Pulling
	Into and from an abyss or an abbey
	carrying a spirit of light, against light itself

This is left
	A poster on a pole in a blizzard of noise

A Bottle
	Half emptied of the half filled reason of life
	drunk in uncertainty with intention, against intention itself

A Mast
	Naked in the twilight shimmering gold
	holding forth in wind against holding itself

A Yellow Dress
	Rumbled in the corner of a store where
	nothing is bought, nothing sold, nothingness itself

A Suitcase
	Carefully packed and abandoned on the steps of some plat
	form destined for obscurity, against obscurity itself

A Loudspeaker
	Amplifying hope, or a warning
	blaring ceaselessly against cessation itself

Love Pulling
	Beyond the false need of definition
	or explanation, love itself against love

This is left
        A shoe soul down on uneven pavement

A Pregnant Women
        Sitting opposite a window carrying silver

A Flashing Light
        Clearing a space of color and purpose

A Watch
        Worn between times accumulating, against accumulation

Love Pulling
        The ceiling into an opening from which you can look out

Oh you have strained so hard to see this last seeing

A Roof
        Glittering in twilight or is it sunrise
        where light catches just the right way, against catching itself

A Crane
        Set up in the distance looming wearier
        with each sound passing slipping against slipping itself

A Floor
        From which you lean into the future holding
        the seam wide open disappearing into the seam itself

Love Pulling
        Being felt as a subtle vibration
        a gentle turbulence mounting, against mounting itself

This is left
     A lonely seed in a far away vault

A Snow Covered Mountain
     Melting before our eyes in the eclipse of reason
     as reason loses its own race, reasoning against itself

A Logic
     Spoken in absolute disbelief of logic
     speaking deafly in defiance against defiance itself

A Can
     Wooden-sided and green grasping
     that what is forgotten piling still, against forgetting itself

A Floating Shirt
     Shifting in an unseen breeze
     emptying the air from the air itself

A Memory
     In constant re-creation in an imagined space
     from where it never was as now, against now itself

Love Pulling
     From the unimaginable dark
     where darkness reveals light against darkness itself

This is left
	A street emptied of purpose

A Dock
	Stranded in the waiting for ships that will never come

A Train
	Lost on a track of hurrying time

A Tunnel
	Into which you run swallowing light, against light

Love Pulling
	From the other side of reason
	motioning you to follow against motion itself

Oh how you can feel it from somewhere just below sense pulling

A Bird
	Walking past benches searching
	flight or rhythm, rhythm against itself

A Steel Cover
	Hiding contents from spilling into the wide open
	expanse of collapse, against collapse itself

A Leather Strap
	Holding back the breaking
	unfolding into unfolding itself

Love Pulling
	This moment into a future now
	already contained in the past, against past itself

This is left
>	A spoon stranded in the bends of time

A Leaf
>	Floating from free fall upwards
>	against seasons as seasons themselves

A Ditch
>	Stumbled upon in the search
>	channeling rain and ice against channeling itself

A Dome
>	Rising from unseen forces forcing
>	a tower to shrink back, shrinking against itself

A Chimney
>	Choking in its own ash strewn
>	in the midst of memory, memory against itself

A Stem
>	Straining to get through its silence
>	signaling time's hope abandoned, abandoned against itself

A Newspaper
>	Carelessly tossed in the folds of silver
>	where elements combine against combining itself

A Coin
>	Whose head is no longer remembered
>	celebrating a victory which is a loss against losing itself

Love Pulling
>	This way and that opening into
>	the pull of the fold of the vibration of love its

This is left
        A half folded umbrella half opened in time

A Clock
        Ticking down the minutes left
        where leaving has stopped itself

A Stuffed Animal
        On a shelf in a park where no one looks

A Charm
        Dangling in a necklace on a string already cut

Love Pulling
        As a door nearly closes on the step
        from which you leap against leaping itself

Oh the fate you seek so hard in the faith you have created

A Bell
        From which no sound rings for no one

A Bench
        In a half remembered dream near a lake on the outside
        of hope where you cannot sit, sitting against itself

A Rail
        Glistening in the sunlight of dead night
        layered with crumbs and direction against direction itself

Love Pulling
        From this place near the end of convention
        a scattered gathering of thought against thought itself

This is left
	A drum in an ocean of drowning sound

A Gift
	Of gratitude in the soundless sound of want
	passed on from hand to hand in opening, opening itself

A Button
	Clasping the endless sides of coasts
	lapping wave after wave of flow, flowing itself

A Machine
	Hidden in the corner thinking
	where thinking spins and laughs, laughing itself

A Pain
	from some dark spot nearly hidden
	in the moment of forgetfulness, forgetting itself

A Seat
	cushioned with longing throwing back
	the back of decline, declining against itself

A Shoe
	taking its own walk in an emptied forest
	of forsaken song singing, against itself

Love Pulling
	This note into being, being written
	in the wide open of what's closing, closing against itself

This is left
    A phone made of a hand never ringing

A Book
    Closed against itself written for no one

A Compass
    of forgotten direction pointing no where

A Scarf
    on the face of surface defining depth and its lack

Love Pulling
    Against all seasons of hatred into love itself
    without saying, saying against itself

*Oh, these days where you want to hide, while retreating into
    the memory of a time that never was*

An Empty Feeling
    Where you long to hold onto
    a so desperate image of a memory, memory against itself

A Bird
    walking slowly into flight
    where flying itself stalls, stalling against itself

A Smile
    Held in a frozen layer of regret
    opening a hole to be filled, filling itself

Love Pulling
    Quietly this time of solace
    seeking peace, peace against itself

This is left
    A blank page calling for a new start

A Broken Pen
    Lasting in the last pocket of time inked black

A Reminder
    That permanence is an illusion, illusion against itself

A Need
    for a form of governance of reason
    reasoning from the heart, the heart itself

A Buckle
    nearly closed to the emptiness of emerging eyes
    in the chill of clasp, clasping against itself

A Glance
    from the side of suspicion holding
    to distance where distance is not yet glancing itself

A Tourist
    on a train with a map of illusion
    rolling in a language and symbol, symbol against itself

Love Pulling
    Like a leftover on a stove in the basement
    of a kitchen baked all night and ready, readiness itself

This is left
	A direction that doesn't know itself

A Jewel
	Hanging from an ear that cannot listen

A Red Band
	On the wrist of the unknown wearer

A Purpose
	So long sought in route, the route against itself

Love Pulling
	Like a wild animal where both wild and animal are
	recognized for themselves and fear is tamed and let free

*Oh how deeply you resonate when the truth is released
	and some sky opens*

A School
	where the desks have given up on purpose and chairs hold
	hope where hope grows, growing against itself

A Guard
	Retired from duty sitting on some beach
	staring down the setting sun, setting against itself

A Window
	Half opened in the dark dawn
	of smell marking memory, memory against itself

Love Pulling
	from the red roof tops glimpsed while landing
	in the lap of warmth from coldness, coldness against itself

This is left
	A young immigrant strapped into desperation

A System
	comprised of meaningless and arbitrary rules
	complicating simplicity, simplicity itself

A Code
	Replacing value made from the actions themselves
	into an increasing abstraction, abstraction itself

A Fear
	Completely manufactured as a means of control controlling
	even the means of manufacturing the fear, fear against itself

A Red Flag
	Jutting out from a green lawn fading
	into orange hoping for white, white against itself

A Leaf
	hanging on the last stem branching
	a corner near a rug thrown against throwing itself

A Fence
	Dividing time in two separating yards
	from a house with no owner, owning against itself

Love Pulling
	from the heart of the matter by
	the matter that matters most now, now itself

This is left
        A rabbit on a path near a woods lost

A Sensation
        of a feeling no longer felt

A Slipping
        off in space somewhere in between

A Pile
        of things no longer needed no longer desired, desire itself

Love Pulling
        Like a shot in the dark
        bracing tightly to what must be let go, letting go itself

Oh how you feel the loss coming before the past

A Sleeping Child
        Safe in the comfort of dream, dreaming itself

A Basket
        Hung carelessly in the corner of a dream
        nearer to wake than wake itself

A Net
        Loosely wove yet steady in the face of storms storming on
        and on against warning, warning itself

Love Pulling
        like a mop or a broom tossed
        in a closet half closed, against closing itself

This is left
	A confusion clearly stated in the wide open of media

A Promise
	Never tested nor talked down being believed as fact
	as if the act itself is truth, truth against itself

A Swollen Belly
	Washed up upon a barren shore of hope
	glittering in the new day light against light itself

A Performance
	As any act of art where art is the way out
	or into that which never left leaving against itself

A Village
	At the outskirts of time
	on a hill near a valley green, green against itself

A Gathering
	Of those still yet believing or believing
	to be looking in conversation, conversation itself

A Law
	Written in old code enforced with thread
	weaving functionality with brutality, brutality against itself

Love Pulling
	From the pages of unwritten future stories to the stories
	we tell ourselves for comfort, comfort against itself

This is left
      A system of systems too tangled to unfold

A Desire
      From an unheard place insisting on being

A Method
      Being handed on regardless of results

A Social Code
      So entwined with actions that independence is crushed

Love Pulling
      or trying to pull us back from the outer edges of the last
      ring of being before being vanishes, vanishing against itself

Oh how hard some try while others push back the pushing on

A Transition
      from one stage to the next in too small steps to transition
      in time to make a difference against difference itself

A Pump
      on the handle of a well so far dry
      that rocks give water, water against itself

A Wheel
      Lost in the spokes balancing uphill
      towards a slanting light, light against itself

A Brick
      from the last roof of the last wall
      of the last fire, fire against itself

Love Pulling
      in so sensible sound that the music
      itself is music as music against itself

This is left
        A wooden pallet on wheels

A Ball Bearing
        Rolling not so smoothly on uneven rails heading straight
        on a track through crooked paths healing itself

 A Pallbearer
        holding the last handles of hope
        interred in the future of reverence, reverence itself

A Dance
        Spinning in the centuries so close
        to merging and transcendence, transcendence itself

A Spring
        taut with coiled reflections of mirror
        the eyes seeing backwards from the glance itself

A Shoot
        Newly formed in ancient ground
        reaching for the stars stranded in sight, sight itself

A Song
        from the song of songs yet to be sung from the highest mounts
        to the lowest valleys now underwater singing, singing itself

Love Pulling
        as if all mattered no matter how small this nearly perfect
        pitch in nearing blackness, blackness against itself

This is left
    A small patch of light

A Blue Mark
    Painted between the cracks near the grass

A Cable
    Being strung between towers and their opposites

A Bush
    Staining to get through the haze in which it stands

Love Pulling
    Like separate strands of the same fabric worn by all and
    addressed by few and rarely noticed, noticing itself

Oh how hard you have tried to sneak a peek into that
    that's peeking back

A Soda Bottle
    On the side of a one lane country road
    near a gas pump empty, empty against itself

A Potted Plant
    Straining from seed to sea
    where light gets through calling, calling itself

A Gravel Road
    Winding through nowhere in particular
    longing for a home or help held homeless itself

Love Pulling
    from the place of past so close
    to now it chokes back tears, tears tearing against tears

This is left
    Good advice from forgotten wisdom

A Whisper
    from somewhere just behind the left ear
    nearly inaudible but still just barely heard, listening itself

A Tub
    full of water and bubbles evaporating
    before our eyes like smoke, smoke against itself

A Tail
    on a nearly extinct animal
    wagging against extinction itself

A Tunnel
    in a desert or a mountain once full of treasure
    depleted in a blink of an eye, blinking against itself

A Twig
    Snapped underfoot in the dry bleaching sun
    so near fire it burns into dust, dust against itself

A Cinder
    from the last ash to which you return blackened from fear
    and white as a ghost, a ghost against itself

Love Pulling
    from the very rich blackness
    where everything is found, finding itself

This is left
    A tire of deflated use in an empty lot

A Gunshot
    Heard by no one that makes all the difference

A Parking Space
    Filled with disuse and open to all

A Cord
    Wound strung from end to end measuring disgust

Love Pulling
    From the vary brink annihilation into the fulfillment
    of distance's collapse, collapsing itself

*Oh to have traveled the full journey now coming to the
    end of the road*

A Deep Sigh
    Heard by on one but felt to the ends of the Earth
    and back as an echo, echoing itself

A Beat
    From the drum of healing to a sea where each wave
    is the vibration of the beat, beating against itself

A Reach
    from open arm to open arm extended
    into the unseen trust, trusting against itself

Love Pulling
    A so simple reply to each whyof being is being
    pulled back to pulling against itself

This is left
    A drop of blood letting go

A Menu
    Written in unreadable script tossed casually on a beach
    abandoned, abandoning itself

A Video
    On a broken screen reflecting half
    of what was recorded, recording against itself

A Bead
    fallen from a string wanting to be a necklace
    strung haplessly around a broken neck, breaking itself

A Space
    between here and there feeling both sad and empty
    filling a void of vacancy, vacancy itself

A Log
    Fitted with moss stacked against a wall letting air
    in between living and the dead, dead against itself

A Sling Shot
    Aimed into higher aspirations
    taken by the hand and handed loss, loss against itself

Love Pulling
    from the park to some higher arc of a half circle
    which you yourself complete, completeness itself

This is left
    Twin branches in the sun

A Waterfall
    Drying up loudly in the heat

A Twist
    in an unwritten plot told nonetheless

A Dragon
    Guarding some entrance mistaken as exit

Love Pulling
    From the smell of something ripe
    into the smell of something other, smell itself

Oh how far and wide into phase shift that you are lost

A Barricade
    strung by rope twisted in holding
    back the flow, flowing against itself

A Stride
    into or against motion
    where motion stops, stopping against itself

Love Pulling
    Like a wrench in too tight grip
    gripping for dear life, life against itself

This is left
    The vacant feeling after a loss

A Tone
    resonating from the last vibration of the last note of the last
    song before the lights come on strongly lighting itself

A Nod
    like a quick wink of the head
    to the next generation arising, arising against itself

A Degree
    certifying nothing but stupidity
    earned with sweat, sweating against itself

A Double Vision
    seen from the side
    like a fog of haze in heat, heat against itself

A Thought
    held against itself while thinking
    in the middle of reason, reason against itself

Love Pulling
    to try to make sense of nonsense
    and what is left to hold, holding itself

This is left
    A bird with a silk scarf

A Lock
    Left open on a closed door

A Mystery
    But not so secret that everyone discovers

A Median
     Through which we relearn how to speak
     and hear each other

Love Pulling
    In the rays of a beam of sun
    that holds all colors, all energies, energy itself

Oh how close to the edge of the edge of being you are found

A Promise
    of a tomorrow without rain but
    where rain is needed, rain against itself

A Campaign
    Spaced out in the time of time
    designed not to open but to close, closing against itself

A Disagreement
    Around the real of the real
    being questioned as illusion falls, falling against itself

Love Pulling
    from a space from a not too distant near
    what can only be sensed, sensing itself

This is left
       A dust cloud from long ago

A Wing
       Rising from ash in the dusk
       clearing and carrying a blessing, blessing against itself

A Statement
       from no certain state other than emptiness
       resounding in near ease, easing against itself

A Prayer
       on the lips of the too earnest
       being recited as a hymn, the hymn itself

A Cap
       Covering the escaping of a gas from where the gas
       is not and changing, changing against itself

A Cell
       Dividing and reforming as the same where wholeness
       and home are found whole, whole against itself

A Ploy
       Trying to evolve into a plot
       which would teach, teaching itself

Love Pulling
       From the least expected source
       suddenly manifesting into the right there, there itself

This is left
	A hushed memory in a crowded train

A Tomb
	Emptied of the secrets it once held

A Refugee
	In the hold of a ship hoping for a plane

A Grill
	On a window facing a brick wall

Love Pulling
	in a scream of a shadow
	near a fire warming cold hearts, heart against itself

*Oh how you search that space created by what shouldn't
	have left*

A Sock
	in a gutter trying to take away a pain
	created from the pair divided, divided against itself

A Snap
	created by the pop of a pop
	in an abandoned room resonating, resonating itself

A Bee
	in mid-flight from itself stranded
	half way between form and transition, transition itself

A Dragon
	guarding the entrance of an exit
	where you stand, standing against itself

Love Pulling
	Like the resolution of a trap
	of a puzzle solved, solving itself

This is left
      The last strand of a beach disappearing

A Number
      On a side of building
      where no one lives, living against itself

A Twig
      Whittled in the absence
      carelessly tossed in a fire, fire itself

A Caravan
      Traveling in ancient light noiselessly gliding across
      the sand dissolving, dissolving itself

A Hushed Conversation
      In a stairwell of the side of a wish
      folded into a wing learning to fly, flying itself

A Puddle
      On a sidewalk of a walking path
      above the trees in the air, the air itself

A Backyard
      of a house on a street going nowhere killed
      with pesticides learning to love the pests, the pest itself

Love Pulling
      Towards you and me and on Earth
      as in heaven as a prayer, praying itself

This is left
> An ancient hum in the vibration of a wave

A Cracking Voice
> In the static of a radio that won't tune

A Web
> Spun in a dusty corner in the light hiding

A Canopy
> Losing mass in the wild of a lost wish

Love Pulling
> from an ocean away near the bottom
> of the Earth to the top of a mountain, the mountain itself

*Oh to be in that place of peace away from the push in the
stillness itself*

A Stroller
> Being pushed by a little girl
> like a doll on vacation free, free against itself

A Seat
> on an abandoned bicycle rusted
> to a lock on a chain on an iron fence, the fence itself

A Rattler
> from the hand of a child crying
> gently in the flight from freedom, freedom itself

Love Pulling
> Like a suitcase on its own trip
> packed and loaded, loaded against itself

This is left
    The breaking of a broken promise unfolding

A Shock
    of the morning news waking
    the sleep from the sleep sleeping itself

A Cry
    in a foreign yet familiar language
    like a whimper in a fog, fog itself

A Map
    on the back of a paper
    yellow with time and thought, thought itself

A Fingernail
    Chipped into pieces like cloth
    worn haphazardly in the dark, dark itself

A Ghost
    in socks slowly walking a path
    planted with flowers rising, rising against itself

A Memory
    from a never forgotten moment
    of an instant that never happened lost, lost against itself

Love Pulling
    like a torch in the hand
    of a beam on the water, water itself

This is left
	A stage waiting to be filled

A Pamphlet
	with old words making little sense

A Compass
	with no true direction of North

A Blouse
	Blowing in the wind on a line held

Love Pulling
	Back from the very brink of an edge
	near a knife to the heart, the heart itself

Oh how you've ransacked the ruing in the search for the key
	to a door already open

A Tingle
	from the first wave of the vibration
	of the echo from the start, starting against itself

A Folding
	into and out of form collapsing
	in upon the opening of us, our us against itself

A Hole
	of pure black light where light is absent
	thus marking a moment, a moment itself

Love Pulling
	This way and that like a marker
	half remembered half held, held against itself

This is left
	A wounded bird hiding in a bush

A Rope
	hung from a cord between two poles
	attached to a bucket empty, empty against itself

A Lace
	from a different century
	lasting from a wanting, wanting itself

A Bell
	Pealing from a tower in place of a church
	near the sea dying, dying against itself

A Raindrop
	falling upward into an extinction
	of time where upwards is against itself

A Balloon
	Abandoned on a beach with a string
	next to a tree where the tree cries, crying against itself

A Dragon
	Awakening in a mountain on a hill
	without a doubt, doubting against itself

Love Pulling
	into and off a side of a slope
	so simply held and released, releasing against itself

This is left
        A rocket launched in a fog

A Crowd
        of one on the ledge of a bridge

A Glare
        from a dying star arising fast

A Formation
        Lined up and ordered, ordered against itself

Love Pulling
        Like footsteps of a race
        run and finished before the start, starting against itself

*Oh how hard you have held despite the grip loosening
        the hold itself*

A Report
        Written as a warning in invisible ink
        read by on one yet talked of often, talking itself

A Repetition
        of an event in memory
        that never happened, happening itself

A Closet
        full of thoughts and numb feelings
        entered into in the dark, darkness itself

Love Pulling
        As if ever there was a more urgent time
        for compassion and peace, peace against itself

This is left
    Pock marks of an assault

A Comprehension
    of a deed in place of peace
    sealed with hot oil, oil against itself

A Disbelief
    Like facts in reverse of meaning
    repeated into belief, belief against itself

A Randomness
    perfectly ordered in hindsight
    where sight is blind, blind against itself

A Dove
    startled from a bush on a ridge
    near a tide less sea shallow, shallow against itself

A Lighthouse
    without a lamp off a coast
    in the receding waters, water against itself

A Tide Pool
    hidden among the rocks
    of a revealed shore near a beach stranded, stranded itself

Love Pulling
    from this perch of a hill
    overlooking the sun setting, setting itself

This is left
    A tower and no height

A Kneeling
    of a young woman smoking in the crouch of a door

A Crosswalk
    Painted black forgotten in the traffic

A Passion
    in a yellow silk dress pulling itself up

Love Pulling
    Against itself fighting for dear life as the veil slightly
    opens and slightly closes, closing against itself

Oh, the race that is the time that is left and the time that divides

A Blue Sky
    Like a half remembered painting
    hung in a closed museum haunting, haunting itself

A Sail
    moving in a port without a boat
    showing the wind's direction, direction against itself

A Berry
    Crushed underfoot on a wall
    littered with meaning, meaning itself

Love Pulling
    So clearly the only source only reason
    to be here on the edge, the edge itself

This is left
	A rage erupting unexpectedly

A Scattered Hope
	like a flight into a peace
	lost in the giving, giving against itself

A Shade
	Pulled against too bright light
	before the dawn, dawn against itself

A Glove
	Lying in the alley behind a park
	lost or found in colors, color itself

A Sandal
	on the foot of a homeless man walking
	through a fog of music, music against itself

A Rock Tower
	Like a beacon of stone quarried
	with flint dug from the past mined, mined against itself

A Hug
	held so desperately close
	the blood nearly stops, stopping against itself

Love Pulling
	As loyal as a dog on a leash less walk
	guiding the way, the way itself

This is left
	An empty house newly cleaned

A Shakiness
	Like a withdrawal and hives

A Routine
	Keeping meaning from falling away

A Doubt
	that certainty is worth keeping

Love Pulling
	into and back without a certain direction
	to pull itself from itself, itself itself

*Oh to stay in a certain sense of sanity just barely there
	and necessary*

A Mirage
	taken as real from the back of memory
	so close you can nearly touch it, touching itself

A Stare
	from a survivor of the edge of a park
	in new sunlight, sunlight against itself

A Rat
	scurrying in a glimpse between bushes
	planted in the hope of flowers rotting, rotting itself

Love Pulling
	just like that fleeting in an instant
	like the loosening of a grasp, grasping itself

This is left
    The sensation and not the thing

A Belt
    on the last notch on the last rung pulled so tight
    that air disappears, disappearing against itself

A Scent
    Like broken flowers releasing
    into the air of the last bee smelling, smelling itself

A Microbe
    undetected and uncared for
    yet vital uncovered in the soil, soil against itself

A Swarm
    or large gathering of what's not supposed to swarm
    thus last attempts for survival, survival against itself

A Father
    in the hand of a little child
    in the back of a dim hall rising, rising itself

A Distraction
    Clear as a clue for the puzzle coming together and
    coming apart wholly, wholly against itself

Love Pulling
    Like the click of a can in resounding sound
    reverberating like the beat of a heart, a heart against itself

This is left
     The last flicker of light off a wave

A Watch
     stranded on a bloodless wrist

A Speech
     Given with hatred disguised as hope

A Line
     Taut between two poles strung in abandonment

Love Pulling
     at the back of something about to take form where you
     watch for appearance, appearance against itself

Oh how much you long for the longing tself to disappear

A Forge
     Stoking the last iron of the last anvil
     standing ready to be replaced, replacing against itself

A Wrapper
     tossed from a package carelessly
     floating in a gutter flooded, flooding itself

A Shuffle
     from this to that like a pack
     running free in the night, night against itself

Love Pulling
     heard faintly from a distance
     so close and followed, following itself

This is left
	A slow stride of a mother and daughter

A Container
	emptied from use holding nothing
	washed up on a shore waiting, waiting itself

A Calmness
	near the center of the swirl
	going straight through the crooked, crooked against itself

A Point
	at the zero not going from here
	to there, but there, there itself

A Droplet
	clinging to a wall rolling slowly
	to extinction, extinction against itself

A Triade
	washing in upon a major storm
	in the early morning running, running against itself

A Grimace
	from some center long ago forgotten
	returning into form, form against itself

Love Pulling
	from the page of history being written
	or returning, or forgetting, forgetting against itself

This is left
     The cool shade of a tree on fire

A Refugee
     Clinging to a paper in the shape of a boat

A Prayer
     from the lips of a dead seed

A Connection
     of a broken line painted in the dark

Love Pulling
     so close to death and grasping
     that in the dying is the living found, finding against itself

*Oh how hard you hang to broken logic which needs to be
     fully broken, breaking itself*

A Tile
     painted from the roots of color
     shinning at dawn, dawn against itself

A Wire
     Carrying news from distant planets
     coming close in the vibration, vibration itself

A Vindication
     Assured from the start waiting
     in wide open holes of wounds, wounding against itself

Love Pulling
     Like a fresh new day of
     a new month noted anew, anew itself

This is left
	A disbelief despite the knowing

A Roar
	from some engine of uncertainty
	parking near the absurd, absurd against itself

A Taking
	grasped in the non-compassionate grasp
	of an unthinking motive, motive against itself

A Ploy
	in the power of unsung harmony
	without a choir, a choir against itself

A Spinning
	of an unfolding plot yet to be revealed
	but already written in acts, acts itself

A Mosaic
	patterned in the wash of rain water
	on a leaking sidewalk talking, talking itself

A Twin
	alone in a cave exploring
	the connection of depth, depth itself

Love Pulling
	from the pain of truth revealed too fast
	to the higher frequency accorded, according itself

This is left
        The last shelter under the leafs of a tree

A Safe Place
        Created by a community of friends

A Meal
        Served upon a plate of openness

A Dust Storm
        Blowing in the eye of a blind wish

Love Pulling
        like loud footsteps in the dark
        rapidly approaching from the back, back against itself

Oh how hard and fast you tried to run only to arrive there,
        where you're from

A Clap
        of disparate sound fading into white
        like a branch or twig in struggle, struggle itself

A Store
        on a railway line of an abandoned highway
        stocking memories from a time passed, passed itself

A Thunder
        Like a loudspeaker close to the ear
        announcing the departure, departure against itself

Love Pulling
        on this night aching to be free
        from the shackles of ignorance, ignorance against itself

This is left
	The rapids sounding in the near distance

A Trust
	of new strangers so seemingly close
	as if connection continued, continued against itself

A Whitecap
	into the new surf arising again
	from the barren suddenly blooming, blooming itself

A Hope
	from the last possible moment
	arriving just in time, arriving itself

A Paper Hat
	Folded on the dusty grass marking
	a happier time of children's games, games against itself

A Raven
	flying in the mind unseen
	marking nothing, nothing itself

A Piece
	Left out in the rain of emptiness
	understanding the waiting, waiting itself

Love Pulling
	just like the peaceful sound of a stream
	glittering in the new morning's sunlight, light itself

This is left
      The sound of paws on a new lawn

A Look
      Anticipating the snatch of a sudden grasp

A Spiral
      Inscribed in the vastness of a shell

A Repetition
      Cycling from the start echoing in the now

Love Pulling
      Like playing puppies in the transition
      of this time between the trap and the release

*Oh you hard you tried to be caught there between the spark
      and the flame*

A Missing
      Like a regret not yet formed
      on an isle of forgiveness, forgiving itself

A Direction
      Outside of compass points
      reaching to the unknown knowing, knowing itself

A Searching Look
      So deeply into the eyes of another
      where both live in recognition, recognition itself

Love Pulling
      into and from the eternal
      rising again into light, light itself

This is left
    The sharp bark of a nearby cut

A Leaning
    of a folded umbrella hanging
    on a table in a dew covered start

A Clothesline
    measuring the time between wash and fold
    strung out like a hope hoping against itself

A Lantern
    Shining from the wicked of past ways swinging
    on a precarious hinge rusting, rusting against itself

A Lesson
    from an unexpected space falling
    into the hold of your hands open, op against itself

A Feather
    fallen next to a table on the grass in a look of a flower
    or folded napkin crumbled, crumbled against itself

A Meeting
    of a new close friend never seen
    like a phantom of thought, thought itself

Love Pulling
    on the last days into lasting
    of a fasting being and dying, dying against itself

This is left
    The kindness of waiting in bed

A Gap
    That fills with the creativity of not wanting

A Connection
    So far beyond words that only vibration is felt, feeling itself

A Completion
    From the other side of the other half, other itself

Love Pulling
    you back for the brink of elimination
    into a resonance shinning in first light, light itself

*Oh for how many days how many years you have waited
    beyond pain beyond this world, this world against itself*

A Lilly Pad
    Struggling against a rising tide
    in a stream of hope, hoping against itself

A Cattail
    Stalking a new day waiting for sun
    in the darkness of the sun singing, singing against itself

A Motor
    of an outdoor bolt roaring quietly
    in the gentle rocking of feeling, feeling itself

Love Pulling
    These words from you to you
    as clear as a cloud breaking, breaking itself

This is left
> A Blue Box in the sand waiting

A Rush
> of waters turning into fire
> growing at the outskirts of lasting, lasting itself

A Creed
> pledged in stone at the bottom of a tree
> demanding a liberation in glass, glass against itself

A Wing
> of the last bird floating on a current
> silently waving goodbye, goodbye itself

A Lineup
> like arranging scattered feelings in the dark
> without eyes to see nor heart to heal, healing itself

A Stalking
> but not with malice defying hope
> with each bite taken in vapor, vapor against itself

A Marching
> ordained from the start slanting
> into a perfection at zero, zero itself

Love Pulling
> in the reflection of a forward gaze perfectly fulfilling
> a gap before the gap opens, openness itself

This is left
> A White Box waiting between what's to come and fulfillment

A Lurch
> Headlong into the void into light sensed

A Rocking
> of the gentle swell of waves cradling a grave

A Scourge
> on the planet of lesser forms disappearing

Love Pulling
> by the lasting hope of love achieved
> at last fronted from the back of light, light itself

Oh how long you have waited for this moment just before
> *breaking to be love, love itself*

A Relic
> from the future past gaining meaning where meaning
> is insignificant and surpassed, surpassing itself

A Task
> from the stooping effort to a heroic call
> on the knees of time bending, bending itself

A Vision
> like an inverted image flying past
> so high and so close it feels right, right against itself

Love Pulling
> Like the joy of a joy so quickly found
> it takes death away into belief, belief itself

This is left
	A Red Box that has always been here waiting to be opened

A Scraping
	of the sound made when the last vibration fades
	into the unsounding from where it arose, arising itself

A Take Off
	on the last runway in the morning light into a setting sun
	rising in the west of forgotten sorrow, sorrow against itself

A Print
	of a lantern on a woman's shirt
	showing the outline of a time to arrive, arriving itself

A Fruit
	with the flower on the inside waiting to be revealed
	on the next to last day running, running against itself

A Tool
	invented out of nothing before a need
	owned by no one for all to share, sharing itself

A Connoisseur
	of water turning into light, sound, waves, the essence and
	not knowing the symbol of beholding and belonging in
	unbroken unity, unity itself

Love Pulling
	As only love can as you and I and all merge into one in this
	vast moment of now is born a new love, New Love itself

This is left

Joe Ross is the author of over fifteen books of poetry, most recently, *History and its Making–The Making of History,* (Bi-lingual French/English, **Presses Universitaires de Rouen et du Havre,** 2017), *1000 Folds,* **Chax Press,** *Wordlick,* **Green Integer Press** (2011) and *Strata,* **DUSIE** (2008). He has also published *Fractured // Connections . . . ,* bilingual Italian/English, **La Camera Verde Press,** *Wordlick* and *EQUATIONS = equals,* **Green Integer Press,** 2004. Former Literary Editor of the arts bi-monthly **The Washington Review** from 1991-1997, and co-founder of the *In Your Ear* reading series in Washington, D.C. and the *Beyond the Page* reading series in San Diego, CA, he received a National Endowment for the Arts Fellowship Award for his poetry in 1997 and the Gertrude Stein Poetry Award in 2003, 2005, and 2006. He lives in Paris.